the comedy of careers

a maha manager's 21 poetically illustrated work
misadventures

ramya rajagopal

- Book Cover Design
- Illustrations Suffixed after each poem
- Complete Presentation

Made in  with love by Ramya Rajagopal

www.mahamanager.in

@mahamanager    

Disclaimer

This is a work of fiction.

Names, characters, businesses, places, events and incidents are either the products of the author's imagination or used in a fictitious manner. Any resemblance to actual persons, living or dead, or actual events is purely coincidental.

The views expressed in this book are personal reflections of the author and do not necessarily reflect any organisational standpoint.

The author's perspectives are individual and artistic.

Feel free to explore the unique perspectives woven into the words and illustrations.

Dedication

To my Ma.
You are the most creative and artistic person I know.
I'm thankful for your genes.

Acknowledgement

I owe it all to my ma and dad, who provided the best - even in tough times.

To my teachers, thank you for shaping my mind and nurturing my curiosity. The writers and poets who crafted worlds within words: your creations have been my one true inspiration. Through books, poems and art, I've become who I am today.

To the folks with whom I cross paths daily, thank you! Each encounter, each conversation, has helped me add colour to my imagination and thoughts.

My travels to distant places and treks to the snow-clad mountains were not just escapes, but chances to learn from various cultures and people. This book reflects my takeaways from those experiences I cherish, depicting the importance of community, conversations, and shared moments.

Thanks to everyone who played a part!

-Ramya Rajagopal

Author's Note

TL;DR:

Hello you! You've made a great choice picking up this book. Reading poetry is so incredibly cool. I have 21 poems for you. It's about all the different jobs I would love to do if I quit my job one day or *shudders* was made to.

Maha means 'Great' in Sanskrit. A Maha Manager follows their calling, not the crowd. Awesome right? Let's go.

Long Version:

This book marks my debut, and what better way to kick it off than with my love for poetry? You'll find 21 of them here. I've spent the past ten years working as a Project Manager, and in the last three years I've been witnessing the job landscape change rapidly. The rise of flexible work, the surge of AI, and the dreaded layoffs—it's been a whirlwind!

All this got me thinking: What if I quit my job one day, or If I *shudders - gulps - tenses* was made to?

I'd love to dive into all those jobs I've always been curious about. Those random gigs that intrigued me, meeting new people, trying new roles—it's all about learning and discovery. Cliché as it may seem, I'm also that kind of nerd who's constantly on a quest to learn new things.

From cafes to weddings, freelance video editing, restaurant work, PR, lifestyle guru, gym manager to working at a florist shop —I would have wanted to give them all a shot.

But this isn't a dramedy; it's real life! And real life is adulting hard and taking on responsibilities—both financial and personal.

So, I did what I know best—I let my imagination run wild and wrote poems.

Some poems are quick reads, while others are a bit longer (I let my thoughts flow here. Do bear with me)

However, this book isn't just about the present. It's about finding what truly matters in the long run. What defines me? What's my big dream? Where do I see myself in the next decade? For me, it's certainly not in a cubicle staring at spreadsheets and BI dashboards but to be an active contributor to solving our everyday problems.

My poems explore the journey of embracing my inherent "maha" or "greatness."

Remember, what I take away from these poems is different from what you do.

Feel free to connect with me at www.mahamanager.in — I'm eager to hear your thoughts.

Cheers and Stay gold!

Ramya Rajagopal

Bengaluru, India (January 2024)

LET'S GO

MAP OF CONTENTS

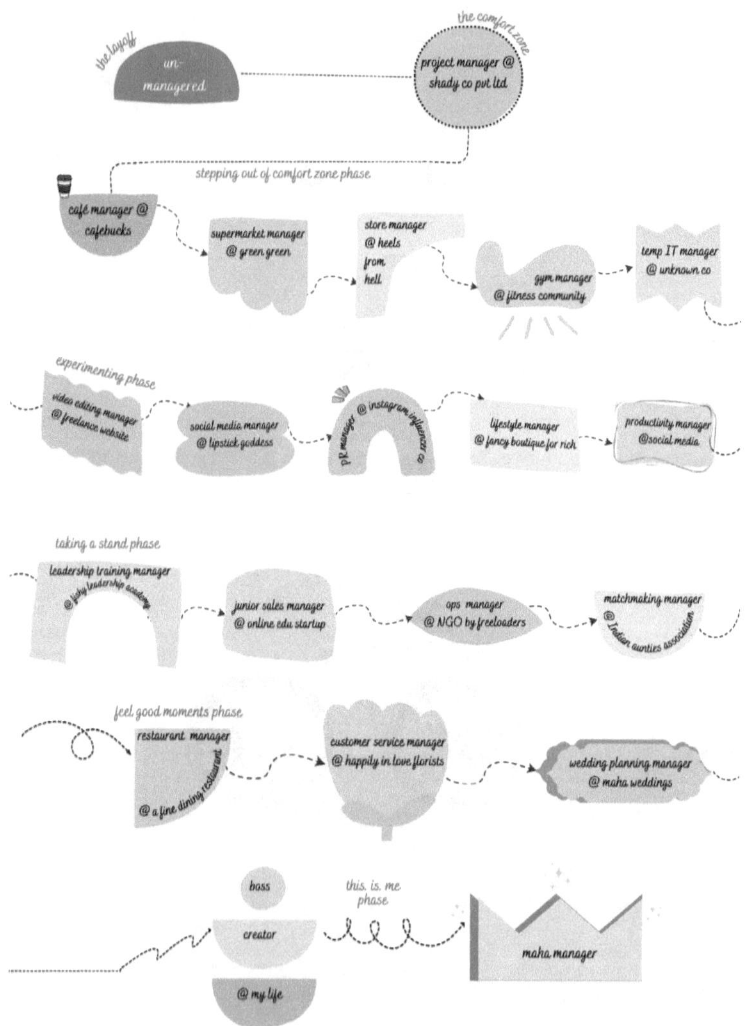

Contents

un-managered

the layoff

un-managered

i was there that morning when the orange sun said hello.
with cold air and calming quiet overflow
then, the singing bulbuls made my garden glow.
and i ended my yogasanas with a bow.

i was there that morning, thanking the universe.
gratitude for everything; happy and adverse.
my phone lit up, distracting my prayers.
and what followed were horrors and shivers!

thank you for your services, it read..
mass layoffs had affected me, they said.
tread lightly with emotions, but wait, why me? i plead
pain in my heart. questions and so many questions in my head
~

"thank you for your services." the email said.

MY NEW SKILL:

MENTAL STRENGTH

project manager @
shady co pvt ltd

the comfort zone

project manager @ shady co pvt ltd

today i'm a project ma-na-ger
mass layoffs are soo ov-er.
this is my do ov-er
my mood, as happy as sum-m-er!

should i instead be a rap-p-er? i thought
perhaps maybe shelf that as an afterthought?
data analysis now let's check-you-out!
oh my my, so many outliers i caught.

these need to be investigated sir
were rules flouted and objectivity blurred?
excellent analysis madam, i concur
but sadly, to us you are a saboteur! a saboteur!

shocked, i blurted, what the actual confusing hell?
his hijacked demeanor turned vicious, i could tell
forget all about this madam and please don't dwell
you're sacked! security, escort her out, he yelled.
~
"thank you for your services." he kind of said?

MY NEW SKILL:

SPEAKING UP

stepping out of comfort zone phase

café manager @ cafebucks

coffee beans scent in the busy air, leaves a mark,
one nervous lady chews an éclair, our café's unique spark.
another old man feeds his beagle a play toy bark,
ah, 'bring your pet to work day,' it is at this business park!

coconut trees to our left, a dull fountain to our right,
our quaint café sits in between, with all its cutesy might.
opens after sunrise all the way till midnight,
our cheesecakes, coffees, and frappes are a five-star delight!

two caffe latte, one decaf flat white,
paneer paninis for a quick bite!
interesting combo, madam - donut with filter-kapee light,
and, was the interview quite alright?

hazelnut aroma dances with conversations, all abound
everywhere,
i hear office romances, dramas, gossip - so much overshare.
'i swear on the caramel pudding, i will quit,' they always declare,
and yet they return the next day, with the same fanfare.

order placed, scanned and paid, drinks poured and drinks to go,
from project manager to making ginger chai & boring cappuccino.
need to get my career back. now! asap! pronto!
"oh here, madame, your exotic mango-mint-crunchy-
cinnamon-choco frappuccino!"
~
"thank you for your services." she excitedly said.

MY NEW SKILL:

HANDLING COMPLEX CLIENT REQUESTS

supermarket manager
@ green green
everywhere

stepping out of comfort zone phase

supermarket manager @ green green everywhere

welcome to green green everywhere!
"the mint leaves are rotting in here."
"ma'am, i have a fresh bunch for you over here."
"no, leaves shouldn't rot. i'm going to shop elsewhere."

dealing with picky customers – this is a pleasant change.
data on spreadsheets, i used to arrange.
now i stare at a welcome poster with an orange,
as i bill and count coins for a change.

"250 a box is too much," he says with disdain.
"sir, these apples were brought from kashmir via train."
"make it 100, i'll buy it now, this is a good bargain!"
ugh hagglers! my annoyance, i couldn't contain.

"sir, you're wearing air jordan shoes to train.
can you stop using the cheap part of your brain?
and appreciate our apple farmers' pain!
250 a box, we have nothing to gain."

"thank you for your services." he embarrassingly said.

MY NEW SKILL:

NEGOTIATION

store manager
@ heels
from
hell

stepping out of comfort zone phase

store manager @ heels from hell

the sign reads, 'heels will heal your feels'.
i snap a pic for my instagram reels.
this place boasts good discount deals.
a shoe store manager, let's see what fate reveals!

'your feet must be adorned with heels always,
walk like models, with sexy sashays.
a big, happy, excited look, your face must portray.
after every sale, don't forget your jumpy hoorays.'

what the actual devil, i mutter,
wearing heels always? my feet will turn to butter!
to try, i was handed a 6-inch stilettos- bold red glitter.
i've always despised this monstrosity! they belong in the sh*tter.

but, i need this job more. "i… love… these," i stutter.
i fall forward as i wobble and flutter,
yoga reflexes kick in, instant anxiety and fear shatter.
i save myself and do a handstand. relieved and unfettered.

the owner stares at me, aghast and bitter.
"here i go, head over heels… " my words scatter.
"madam, we're the new trendsetters,
with this, we create a unique.. client experience.. better?"
~
"thank you for your services." she disappointingly said.

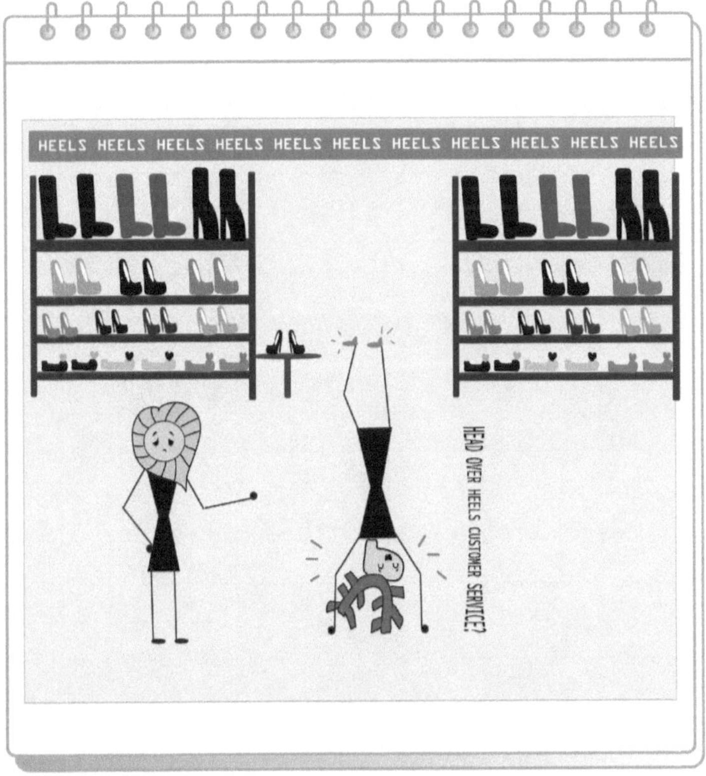

MY NEW SKILL:

THINKING ~~OUT OF BOX~~ HEAD OVER HEELS

stepping out of comfort zone phase

gym manager @ fitness community

ah one, ah two, ah three, ah four,
squat and jump, ladies, squat and jump.
this is torture, i shan't do no more,
dump the slump, ladies, use those muscles to pump!

a fusion of motivation and sweat stink baked,
some are here to get toned and some to get caked.
with so much at stake, willpower cannot be shaked,
plenty many fitness classes to partake; laziness they forsake.

triceps, foreceps, quads, and hamstrings,
i tell myself, this is a temp job, i'm trying, i'm trying.
nobody is hiring now, stick it out even if it's boring,
soon good news will lift me; my career will take off sprinting!

a confused newbie walks in; yoga is fun, but hiit, i shun,
"time to punch it out, muay thai boxing has begun.
also, the sun is out, why don't you go for a run?
and, here is your protein shake, madam, with a choco bun."

a sweaty man grunts, 'i demand a refund! i quit.
i can't do one push up, i'm here to get fit.'
"why don't you try crossfit, and use all your grit?
abandon all self-doubt, whirling in your mental cesspit,
this is your day one, commit; picture your summit."
~

"thank you for your services." they half-heartedly said.

MY NEW SKILL:

HEALTH & WELLNESS MOTIVATIONAL GURU

temp IT manager
@ unknown co

stepping out of comfort zone phase

temp IT manager @ unknown co

grey-walled tiny room in a basement,
paint chips off everywhere, exposing dusty cement.
old laptop with a yucky sticky keyboard, my only equipment!
this temp job is only for my emi payment.
what has happened to my career?! i lament.

my 'trainer' speaks fast, mouth full of wonton.
'click this button, click that button,
password reset's a game of badminton.
other procedure docs are shoved in that carton,
this is all your training; here i pass the baton.'

i.t manager sounds cool,
non-engineer i am, should've gone to tech school.
my self-confidence is swirling in my mental whirlpool,
i hope i don't screw up as a temp and look like a fool!

'my computer doesn't work,'
"do your job," they snark.
irked, 'did you try restarting?' i politely bark,
ugh, i'm dealing with professional idiots, i remark.
these common-sensical asks are a walk in the park!

idiocy and boredom,
obstacles to my financial freedom.
need to start a great plan to build my own kingdom,
i stare at the peeling wall as i eat my rice and papadam.
~
"thank you for your services." nobody, i repeat, nobody said.

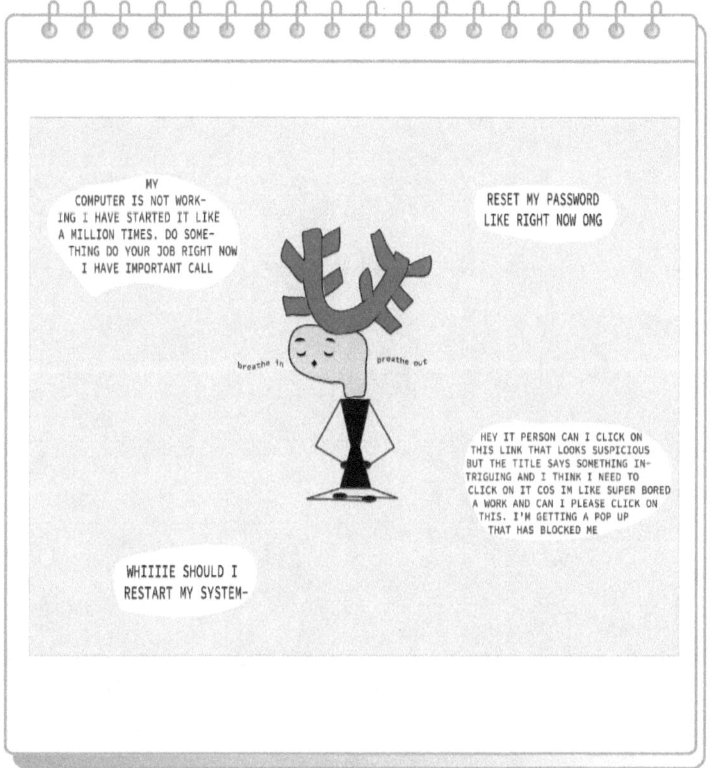

MY NEW SKILL:

PATIENCE

video editing manager
@ freelance website

experimenting phase

video editing manager @ freelance website

fly like a fairy, i want,
four purple wings with a glowing radiant.
also, riding a horse so gallant,
my video intro shall be a 'dope' resonant!

"no, madam," i said, "i can't."
"this video intro will only be an irritant."
"how dare you not follow my orders, you deviant?"
"common sensically, fairies with four wings need not ride
horses, you ignorant!"
~

this edited video, i don't look cool, and i'm quite unhappy.
mrbeast style, why did you not copy?
just two minutes run time; expected twenty - of me chirpy!
here i look quite mopey; overall the algo will deem this sloppy.

sir, four minutes of raw footage you gave me,
"ahhs umms and ohhs" ruled minutes to three.
the rest are special effects to extend the video, you see.
and, mrbeast cleaned the sea, planted trees, and gave things
for free.
your content has nothing like that, i did my best, now pay me
my fee!
~

"thank you for your services." both mockingly said.

MY NEW SKILL:

DEALING WITH COMPLEX DEMANDS

social media manager
@ lipstick goddess

experimenting phase

social media manager @ lipstick goddess

canva-illustrator-photoshop skills i've learnt- i'm awestruck.
typography ideas flow like a beautiful running blackbuck.
'dazzling goddess, yes mondays suck.
try our pinonee'red' lipstick for luck!'

creativity hugs the deadline process;
my brain then turns into a colourful fortress.
this job is cool minus the awful stress;
we all generate content in excess.
new social media trends make us digress;
monday to sunday posting schedules we obsess.

'melon pink for first date is your ultra confidence potion.'
'rendezvous chicas is our gift to girls' night fun with sexy combination.'
'velvet bordeaux on date night will make you the new sensation!'

our motto is all about grabbing attention;
we plant seeds of want, set them in motion.
we play on people's insecurities and all their prevalent emotion,
skillfully wrap them up as the 21st century's empowered ambition.
i disagree; i say. lipsticks always make my day; so let's parley.
bold, beautiful, ready to soar; with words i play.
a bold swipe of my 'ruby blushes' lipstick, i'm ready to slay.
an electrical surge of confidence i feel straightaway!

lipsticks represent more than makeup and vanity - 'kay?
haters with their negative wordplays should walk away.
they are here to stay; usurp the world, trailblazers get ready
to foray.
~

"thank you for your services." my imaginative talking poster
said

ME AS A SOCIAL MEDIA MANAGER

MY NEW SKILL: 3 Cs
CONTENT, COMMUNICATION, CAMPAIGNS

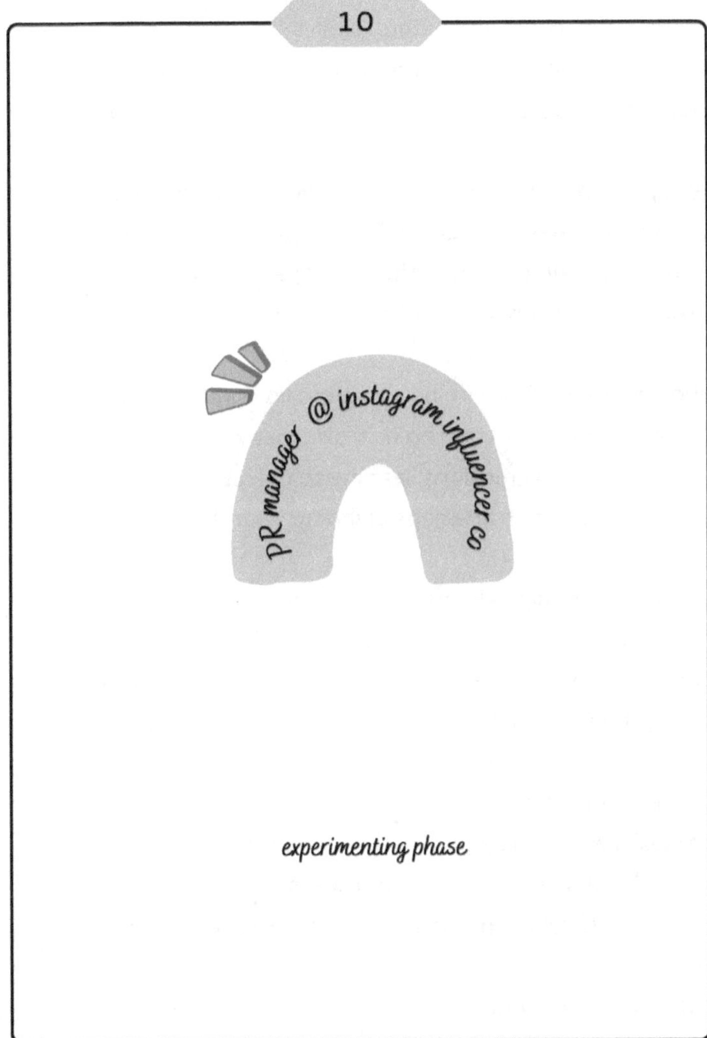

experimenting phase

PR manager @ instagram influencer co

current wealth is not money, but social media followers.
made up of lovers and haters, of all internet users.
influencers now deemed the new movers and shakers,
but one misstep sends their brand down social media gutters!

as a pr manager, i advise, educate, and manage 'em all,
all my client has to do is read my script, sit like a doll.
with captivating content, the public gets enthralled,
i then send my invoice, for her to pay it all.

their lives are filled with he-said-she-said drama and action,
their comments section holds troll's many questions.
these play with emotions, leading to dejection,
i intervene, launch an image clean-up operation.

using my contacts at various media outlets,
'false news! not her brand's personal palette,' i state.
then comes the candid photo-op of her making veggie cutlet,
'look, she's a homebody sweet thing!' critical bullets we negate!

i quit my job, ready to flee.
she asks why. 'this is just not my cup of tea!'
in reality, it's an overload of pettiness to see,
i'm selfishly saving my sanity from disintegrating rapidly!
~

"thank you for your services." she apathetically said.

MY NEW SKILL:
PUTTING OUT (VIRTUAL) FIRES

| 53

lifestyle manager
@ fancy boutique for rich

experimenting phase

lifestyle manager @ fancy boutique for rich

a white studio. white candles. beige lamps.
golden-coloured letters on white posters, hung on a silver clamp.
'life is a mélange of exquisiteness. come here for a revamp!'
and zesty, citrusy scent captivated the room like a champ.

'life is all about confidence!' she says.
in that angelic white chanel dress, she slays.
'we first provide clients with an ubiquitous-holistic-experience, with entrees,
then serve ethereal-synergies along with our best chardonnays.'

too many fancy words; confusion everywhere!
'madam, i find myself in this inescapable quagmire.
what do i exactly do?' i ask, my expression sincere.
'oh darling, we sell lifestyle in a tranquil stratosphere!'

bewilderment overtook my thinking prowess.
using fancy words is this job's role, i assess.
it's all about energies, aromas, and words, i guess?
my inner dr. tharoor's vocabulary, i shall harness.
this is impromptu acting, time for me to be an actress!
~

"thank you for your services." she ethereally said.

ME AS A LIFESTYLE GURU MANAGER

MY NEW SKILL:

SPEAKING FANCY

*productivity manager
@social media*

experimenting phase

productivity manager @social media

arrange your life by accepting things you dread,
i changed my life by following these steps instead.
my five-star tips are here, read this twitter thread,
if you liked what i typed, support me, use your words to spread.

dreams are ready to maximize; wake up before sunrise.
not six or five. but three, it will not work otherwise!
cold water splashed on face, say affirmations to revitalize,
ask the energies, 'advise me, on new ideas for me to capitalize.'

productivity starts with strong mindfulness,
to declutter life; use to-do lists; write all your weaknesses.
order them by priority stat, approach with calm openness,
slow magical new changes, your life shall soon witness.

social media is the god of all rakshasa-diablo-devil.
they say, 'oh, it is free to use; but your time and data is our oil.'
temporary dopamine you get with likes and follows from garboil.
also served with complimentary trolls' turmoil.
to network, it was hailed, and now your self-esteem is in their jail!

saying no is an art to be practised.
people demand for your time, refuse to be enticed.
your time is yours and yours only, do not let it be sacrificed.
Say no to all toxic asks and be satisfied.
~
"thank you for your services." my six twitter followers
deterministically said.

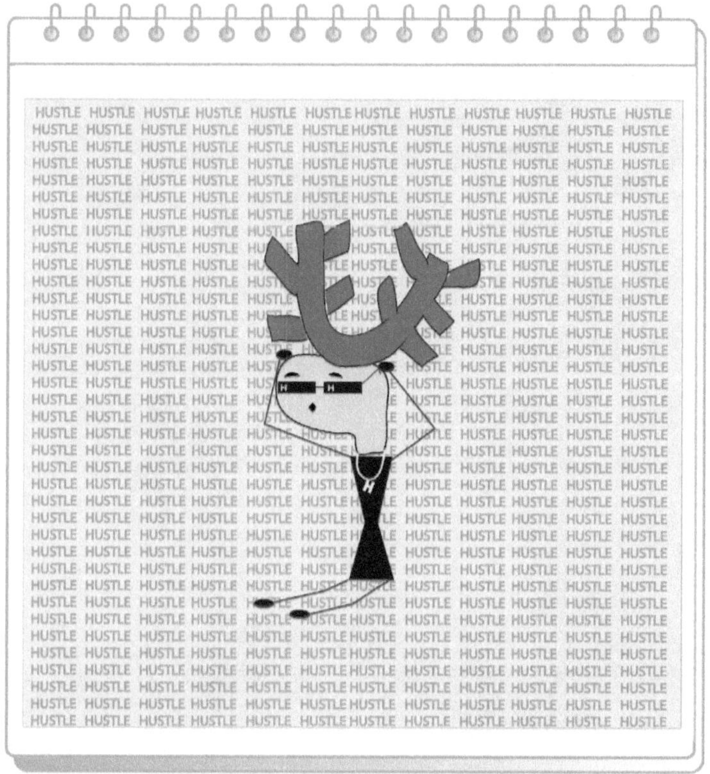

MY NEW SKILL:

COMMUNICATING WITHIN 140 CHARACTERS

leadership training manager
@fishy leadership academy

taking a stand phase

leadership training manager @ fishy leadership academy

soft skills we shall work on,
with our plentiful case studies on successful cons.
we will have an expertly skilled soft-skilled don,
walk away beaming with confidence like a beacon.

you will be a force to reckon with; you're now a leader!
followers will look up to you, waiting for the new world order.
motivation, inspiration, aspiration; buzzwords to use as a guider,
quote nuggets of wisdom from famous people via internet's feeder.
don't speak too much; leave some to imagination; make them ponder.

use emotional stories to touch their feels,
yap about tales of deals that you've sealed.
post snaps of your luxury rented car and some wheels,
tell them making millions is possible; turn up your zeal!

then lead an online leadership academy, of course,
charge them 99 bucks for a mini-course.
add multiple paid brand adverts to endorse,
make them believe you're their only recourse.
this is how you become a millionaire, feel no remorse!
~
"thank you for your services." they expected me to say in their google reviews.

MY NEW SKILL:

SPOTTING SELF AGGRANDISING ‘LEADERS’

junior sales manager
@ online edu startup

taking a stand phase

junior sales manager @ online edu startup

'what is your monthly sales number?'
big boss shouted, Mr. not cool as a cucumber.
'holiday time is slow, let's check after december?
i'll send you the deets boss, i'll remember.'

'i need the number now.
open the excel, filter by month, 1-2-3 show.
you haven't met your quota, wow!
our bottom line has taken a blow.'

'it's unethical, harassing parents.
karma will slap us all, agents.
this is not sales, this is us being serpents,
forcing the middle class with unwanted payments.'

'coercing parents. you are a sick, sick man.
selling subpar products that should face a ban.
your fake online education is a villainous plan.
this business is a sham. i quit this job.' and then i ran.
~

"thank you for your services." nobody said.

MY NEW SKILL:

SPOTTING UNETHICAL EGOTISTS

ops manager
@ NGO by freeloaders

taking a stand phase

ops manager @ NGO by freeloaders

'poor children, we educate,
with wealthy folks, we associate.
our various digital schemes we elaborate,
their altruistic emotions, we navigate,
we love eviscerating their bank accounts!
our actions will not abate.'

'new ipads for girls' education,
the future is female, a vision for our nation.
pre-order rice and wheat for the orphanages to ration,
new roof building fund to save the abandoned from damnation.'
toying with the rich; our guilt-free volition!

all of their under-the-table dealings,
remind me of sick hyenas mauling.
took me a few weeks to see through the fooling,
as their true nature began unfurling.
~
unanswered complaints to the leaders began piling;
my rage and my blood continued boiling.
'rampant corruption's roots continued deepening,
and their nefariousness started unravelling.
their sweet-talking deceits turned gruelling.'

"we are cutting this position, i'm afraid,
please vacate now, and by the end of day, you will be paid."
~
"thank you for your services." the hr devilishly said.

MY NEW SKILL:

SPOTTING FAUX-ALTRUISTIC MANIACS

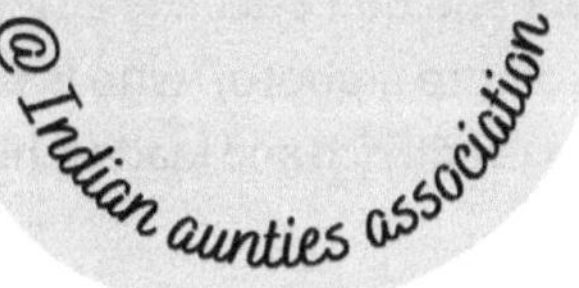

taking a stand phase

matchmaking manager @ Indian aunties association

sandalwood dhoop engulfed the vibrant pink room,
lorry art adorned the wall that said, 'find that groom!'
matches made in heaven don't last, for they bring in gloom,
but indian aunty-approved matches bring 50 shades of bloom.

'so corny!' i laughed out loud, reading the wall.
the ceo aunty appeared, eyes shooting fireballs.
'if you aren't serious, then you may leave the hall.
matchmakers bring happiness and love like a waterfall.'

well, i am desperate for a job.
quick! show respect and don't act like a slob.
'my apologies!' i point to a photo, 'who is this heartthrob?'
"that's our priority 1 client. rich and loaded. his family is the mob."
~

these photos are of women who cannot cook,
and, here are the nerds with noses buried inside a book.
that pile has the unemployed ones, with no outlook.
and, these are the plain looking ones, we refuse to book.
your job is to go through the bio-datas and take a hard look,
give us your analysis of who comes with a fat chequebook!

all the bio-datas you then re-order,
block our next street astrologer's busy calendar.
pay upfront to our in-house face reader,
all important information, you have to consider.
these are heavy responsibilities to shoulder,
do not disappoint me and flounder.
~

madam auntyji, single humans are not data and statistics.
deciding on matches based on physical aesthetics?
these are your old fashioned, sexist, and colourist tactics!

our wedding industry is a game of moral and financial gymnastics.
don't get me started on the mathematics of dowry politics.
i refuse to be a part of this judgemental world of lunatics!
~
"thank you for your services." of course, she never said.

restaurant manager

@ a fine dining restaurant

feel good moments

restaurant manager @ a fine dining restaurant

from pie charts to pushing food carts,
i orchestrate rhythms, plan, and execute all parts.
here's where your five-star fine dining experience starts,
i get to use my smarts, so this place can win your hearts!

the table is my stage, i plan the best for my guests,
display our chef's culinary magic at its finest.
every plate is a customised masterpiece, full of zest,
from the clink of the silverware to the crackle of pans, let's embark on a quest!

from morning till night, the restaurant manager must stay put,
lovers' whispers and old friends' chatter are a beaut.
hush-hush conversations, soft noises, and laughter sprout,
music to my ears, like a conductor of an opera, watch out!

chaos reigns all the time, human egos are indeed frail,
inside the kitchen, stress takes over workers' morale.
outside in the hall; it's a furor over a salad sans sauteed kale.
frenzy and furors impaled, i balance them like the libran scale.
i then make a log in my journal, so i can enjoy my drink and share the tale.

~

"thank you for your services." the customer satisfactorily said.

ME AS A RESTAURANT MANAGER

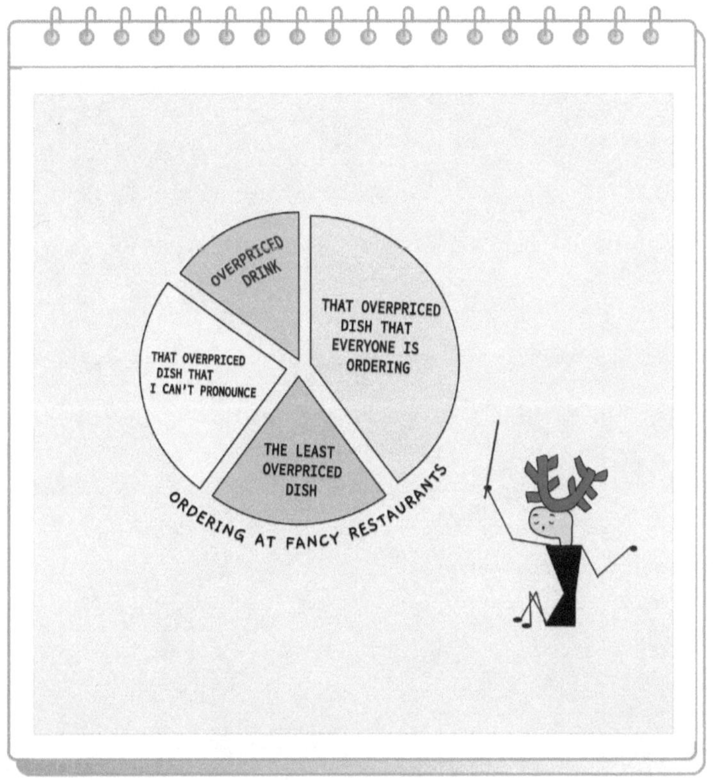

MY NEW SKILL:

SMILE AND NOD

SMILE AND NOD

customer service manager
@ happily in love florists

feel good moments

customer service manager @ happily in love florists

ivory-coloured floral wall, ruby poster announced, customer is king.
petals bloom this fall, ready to dance and sing.
love shall befall you; behold that ring!
this is nature's call, spring, and hearts cling.

tring tring! Bonjour madam!
we make smiles bloom and possible!
a piercing cry! 'can you fathom?
i have been abandoned, my life will fall and crumble
my emotions discarded; my existence denied, shattered and irreparable!'

tring tring tring! hola senor! we make smiles—
'she refused me and the roses! now my heart door closes
memories covered with bruises, my soul's darkness rises.
failed to see our love's many new changes-
the slow shift from unconditional ravages to unrequited wedges.
blithering blind fool i am. curses to me! curses!'

deep breaths darling, deep breaths! time to bid adieu
paint your future, hopeful and nouveau
water your heart with gentle words, sweet as tiramisu.
fight the pain and darkness, like warriors of jujitsu!

pain withers away once it breaks you
breakups happen, excruciating like the flu.
heart always heals, life always blooms, souls always renew.
time repairs all wounds, make mind strong to get through

~

"thank you for your services." they cryingly said.

wedding planning manager
@ maha weddings

feel good moments

wedding planning manager @ maha weddings

ruby gold jhumkas, emerald-studded nosering,
cornsilk saree with pink pearls poppin',
she enters the room, crowds start rejoicing,
Acoustic dynamic stage, five-star catering, ar rahman music energizing.
time to let hair loose, let the sangeet begin and time for some dancin'.

marigolds arches, crowns owned by roses,
lotuses add to the charm; all elegance rises.
every now and then, one or two crisis arises,
we cruise through the bruises, erasing the noises.
the couple sigh with relief, with one or two mild curses,
uhh. the drama and fragile ego of relatives! such pains in our arses.

the sun is up, the bulbuls & other birds create sweet symphony,
the bride all decked up, beauty & elegance in perfect harmony,
the groom looks radiant, standing next to the ebony balcony,
'can't wait to marry my love, put me out of my agony.'
the moony groom's lil speech is so swoony,
'let's start the ceremony of this holy matrimony!'

the married couple have eyes for each other, love so devout.
the caterers do their thing, the gift bags then roll out.
surprised gasps go up in the air, and people shout,
'this is marvelous gift! this wedding was perfection, and you went all out!'
~
"thank you for your services." the couple gleamingly said.

ME AS A WEDDING PLANNING MANAGER

MY NEW SKILL:
DEALING WITH MULTIPLE FAMILY DRAMAS

the 'this is me phase'

boss creator @ my life

i'm closer to figuring out my dream,
working odd jobs never made me once beam.
i did learn new skill sets that fit my theme,
i'm going to head my world! i say this and gleam.

culture, art, handicrafts, exotic stories,
our rich heritage deserves its own new glories.
my love lies with tales from our histories,
my heart belongs to everything art and its backstories.

my future is my canvas, nouveau and oh so exciting.
i intend to lead it to greatness, with creative imprints so exhilarating.
of first dates, first kisses, proposals and weddings so enchanting,
stories of families, stories of jobs, stories of travels, memories everlasting!

i'm a creator. my dream- i helm
i now independently curate artsy items,
for people like you and me, who love to read poems,
of memories shining and glowing like gems,
escaping to a beautiful neverland, far away from this mayhem!
~

"thank you for your services." your review will one day say.

MY NEW SKILL:

TRUSTING THE JOURNEY OF MY AUTHENTIC SELF

the 'this is me phase'

maha manager

being 'great' starts with my mindset,
i'm not my role title; it's good i got a reset.
at jobs, i thought i was an irreplaceable asset,
naivete is blinding, layoffs arrive suddenly, so get set.

maybe i liked these jobs, but it's not truly me,
i wish to use my skill sets to fly and be free,
amidst the clouds where i can see the trees,
feeling my happiness rush to the nth degree.
i must quit, fly high, break this bondage and flee!
~
who is a maha manager, i wondered,
is it someone who is deemed a leader or commander?
is it someone who is a greatness and glory beholder?
or is it someone who has solved world problems as a silent founder?

being 'maha' is a state of mind,
i feel it deep inside my heart's find.
i'm not a buzzword my boss says at my place of grind,
i'm more than others' opinions and role titles that have kept me behind.

i now seek my own personal progress,
embrace my strengths to say hello to my inner goodness.
i build on my skill sets and talents with love and finesse.
i am grateful for the lessons of my career madness,
recognising it was all a process to reveal my limitless greatness!
~

"thank you for your great services." the universe triumphantly said.

ME AS A MAHA MANAGER!

MY NEW SKILL:
CELEBRATING MY UNIQUE 'GREATNESS'

THE END

Dear reader,

Thank you for reading 'the comedy of careers: a maha manager's 21 poetically illustrated work misadventures'.

Share your favorite part of the book with me. The section that brought a smile to your face or made you nod in agreement. Your feedback means the world!

Write to me at themahamanager@gmail.com or DM me on my social accounts.

For more poems on career poetry:

1. If you prefer the audio format: check out my Spotify.
2. If you prefer video format: check out my Youtube.
3. If you prefer the format of visual storytelling: check out my Linkedin or Instagram.

Visit www.mahamanager.in for more details.

Thank you (immensely) for your *reading* services!

Ramya Rajagopal

About the Author

Hello there! I'm Ramya Rajagopal, the person behind these poems.

I'm a big fan of storytelling and the magnetic power of words and visuals. I'm here to express my thoughts and observations about careers, jobs, and work-life using the magic of poetry, visual storytelling, and a bit of humour.

Life's not complete without a good laugh at ourselves, right?

I'm from Namma Bengaluru (India), my home sweet home.

My work-mode-on / 9-5 avatar is where I'm a data analytics-business intelligence - problem solving loving PM.

My work-mode-off / creativity-mode-on / 5-9 avatar is where I'm the most happiest self, creating magic.

When I'm not lost in writing or buried in a book, I keep myself occupied with my creative pursuits as a hobbyist digital illustrator and a Thanjavur artist. I unwind by finding solace in the extremes – from the calmness of meditation to the intensity of MMA.

And when I'm not working on my hobbies, I'm out there exploring as a traveller and a trekker, soaking in the great outdoors, enjoying great food and experiencing different cultures.

Curious to know more? Hop on over to www.mahamanager.in

www.ingramcontent.com/pod-product-compliance
Lightning Source LLC
Chambersburg PA
CBHW021112130726
47988CB00003B/998